For Conor, Kelsey, Jesse and Tasha. Remember when you were little?

Copyright © 2016 Ken Hoehn and Silver Fox Publishing
Second Printing 2018
All rights reserved. No part of this book may be reproduced in any manner whatsoever
without written permission from the publisher and author.

All photographs and text by Ken Hoehn

For inquiries about reproduction rights or purchasing pictures visit www.KenHoehn.ca
for contact information.

Printed in China

ISBN 978-0-9813412-3-1

Contact Ken at the website for copies of his outstanding books about the journey of nature.

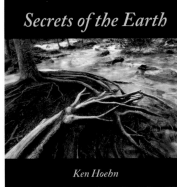

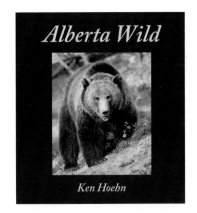

www.KenHoehn.ca

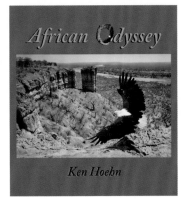

When I was Little

and

If I was Big

Ken Hoehn

wilderness artist

When I was little
I climbed in a tree,
and dreamed all the things
I wanted to be...

Black Bears come in many
colors, from black through
a range of browns, and
sometimes even white.

... a puffin out fishing,

Whoooooooaaaaaaaa

There are three kinds of Puffins in Canada. This is the Atlantic Puffin, from Newfoundland.

Puffins live in colonies and dig burrows in the ground for a safe place to live.

a fox on the prowl,

Why do shadows on snow look blue?

It is from the reflection of the blue sky above on the snow, which is just frozen water.

When foxes play they can look like they are dancing.

Can you dance?

a moose in the willows,

Male Moose grow large antlers on their heads.

Moose sometimes have to kneel down to drink because their legs are so long.

or even an owl!

Who? Whoo?
Me! That's who!

Owls can make
many different
sounds.

The Great Gray Owl
is the Provincial Bird
of Manitoba.

There are big owls and little
owls. This is a Pygmy Owl.

He is one of the smallest.

I learned all my colors,
like red,

When we travel to different places, we may see different birds and animals.
This bird is called the Andean Cock-of-the-Rock. He lives in Peru.

orange,

and blue,

Baltimore Orioles are mostly orange on the front but they are black on the back.

How many blues are there in a Mountain Bluebird?

Lots of birds have white feathers, like this Snowy Egret.

Baby Black Bears learn how to climb trees when they are very young.

and bright
yellow too.

Yellow Warblers like to sing in the spring.

What do you think his song sounds like?

Do you like to sing too?

It is easy to confuse Yellow Warblers with American Goldfinches, shown above.

Can you see how they are different?

As I dreamed, I counted
how many there were,
as the creatures appeared
in their feathers or fur.

Lynx have great big paws
to help them walk across
deep snow in the winter.

They can be hard to see because their
fur looks a lot like their surroundings.

It is called "camouflage" when wild
animals use their colors to hide in plain
sight.

one
pretty kitty cat

two
splashy whales

Humpback Whales sometimes leap out of the water when they play. It is called a "breach" when they do that.

2

Whales have two big tail fins to wave goodbye with as they dive into the sea.

three
friends hiking

3

Dall Sheep are found in the Yukon and Alaska. They have beautiful white coats and live high in the mountains.

four
wary wolves

4

Gray Wolves are never easy to see.

Can you count four?

Wolves have big paws with four toes.

How many toes do you have?
Are you sure?
Better count them again!

five
fluffy bears

These Grizzly Bear cubs have just finished their lunch, and still have their milk moustaches on.

Does that ever happen to you?

Grizzly Bears have five toes that they use for digging.

5

6

six
long legged stilts

Black-necked Stilts have long legs so they can walk around in the water without getting wet. They never have to wear rubber boots!

They stick their legs straight out behind when they fly.

seven
long necks

7

Trumpeter Swans have long necks so they can reach down below the water to find food. They sometimes push their faces right into the mud at the bottom. Yuck!

Swans run on top of the water when they want to take off.

There are not seven in this picture.

8

eight
dashing ducks

Common Mergansers are among the fastest
swimming birds in the world.

Look closely and do not forget to count Mom.

nine

eager eagles

9

Bald Eagles wait for the ocean tide to recede so they can catch little fish left behind in the pools that remain.

Can you see nine?

10

ten
rainbow cranes

Sandhill Cranes have beautiful deep voices.
You can hear them coming from far, far away.

Yes when I was little
I dreamed each and all.
I counted the creatures,
the big and the small.

1, 2, 3, 4, 5, 6, 7

more

Can you count all of these?
I am not sure that I can!

And if I was big,
I would show that I care,

Baby swans are called "cignets". These are Mute Swans caring for their cignet.

And play with my babies,
Like this mother bear.

This Black Bear cub jumped on his mother's head and she gave him a toss or two as he hung on, just for fun!

The next day he was playing with his brother and sister.

I would soar over sadness,
an eagle above...

Bald Eagles are known to fly high in the mountains looking for food.

... and give out my hugs,
to share all my love...

Black Bear cubs like the monkey bars.

Maybe I would take my kids to the playground too,
if I was big.

When I
was little,

and

if I was
big...